Preface

In today's rapidly evolving digital landscape, the ability to transform innovative ideas into functional applications has become increasingly accessible, even for those without traditional coding backgrounds. The emergence of no-code platforms has democratized app development, enabling entrepreneurs, creatives, and professionals from diverse fields to bring their concepts to life without writing a single line of code.

This guide is designed to empower you with the knowledge and tools necessary to navigate the no-code ecosystem effectively. Whether you are aiming to solve a specific problem, launch a startup, or explore new avenues for creativity, this book provides a comprehensive roadmap from ideation to deployment.

Throughout the chapters, you will:

- **Understand the No-Code Movement:** Gain insights into how visual development environments are reshaping the tech industry, making app creation more inclusive and efficient.
- **Plan and Validate Your App Idea:** Learn to conduct market research, analyze competitors, and create wireframes to ensure your concept meets real-world needs.
- **Build Your App Step-by-Step:** Dive into setting up no-code platforms, designing user interfaces, adding essential features, and assessing your app to ensure functionality and user satisfaction.
- **Monetize and Market Your App:** Explore various revenue models, pricing strategies, and marketing techniques to reach your target audience effectively.
- **Scale and Grow Your App Business:** Discover methods to acquire users, automate processes, integrate third-party services, and consider options for expanding your team or selling your app.

By the end of this journey, you will be equipped to not only build and launch your app but also to iterate and improve upon it, responding to user feedback and market dynamics. Embrace the possibilities that no-code development offers and take the first step toward turning your innovative ideas into impactful digital solutions.

Table of contents

Introduction

Why You Do Not Need Coding Skills to Build an App

For many years, developing an app required extensive knowledge of programming languages such as Java, Swift, or Python. However, the digital landscape has evolved significantly, and now, with the rise of no-code and low-code platforms, you no longer need to be a software engineer to bring your app idea to life. These platforms provide intuitive, drag-and-drop interfaces that allow anyone—even complete beginners—to design, develop, and deploy fully functional applications without writing a single line of code.

The traditional approach to app development is often time-consuming and costly, requiring teams of developers and months of iteration before a product is ready for launch. No-code platforms eliminate these barriers, making app development faster, more affordable, and accessible to entrepreneurs, small businesses, and creatives who want to turn their ideas into reality without hiring a developer.

The Rise of No-Code and Low-Code Platforms

The emergence of no-code and low-code solutions has revolutionized the way people approach app development. These platforms are designed to democratize technology, making it easier for anyone to build apps with minimal technical knowledge.

Some of the most popular no-code and low-code platforms include:

- **Bubble** – A powerful visual programming platform that allows users to build complex web apps.
- **Adalo** – A user-friendly tool for creating mobile applications without coding.

- **Thunkable** – A no-code platform that specializes in building mobile apps for iOS and Android.
- **Glide** – A tool that converts Google Sheets into fully functional mobile and web apps.
- **Softr** – A platform that helps users build web apps using Airtable as a database.

The global no-code market is growing rapidly, with businesses and individuals alike recognizing the potential of these tools. According to industry reports, the no-code market is projected to reach over $65 billion by 2027, indicating a massive shift in how software is created and deployed.

Success Stories of People Who Built Apps Without Coding

To further illustrate the potential of no-code app development, here are a few inspiring success stories of individuals and businesses that have launched successful apps without writing any code:

1. **Dividend Finance** – This financial services company used a no-code platform to build their initial app, allowing them to streamline their loan application process and serve thousands of customers efficiently.
2. **Comet** – A freelance marketplace that connects developers and businesses was built using Bubble. This no-code solution allowed the founders to launch quickly and scale their platform without a technical co-founder.
3. **HelloPrenup** – Featured on *Shark Tank*, this platform helps couples create prenuptial agreements online. Built using Bubble, the founders turned their idea into a successful business without any coding knowledge.
4. **Qoins** – A fintech app that helps users pay off debt more efficiently was built using no-code tools. The founders validated their idea and launched their platform without hiring developers, saving them significant costs upfront.

These examples demonstrate that you do not need a technical background to create an app and turn it into a profitable venture. Whether you want to launch a startup, create a side hustle, or build a tool for your business, no-code development opens endless possibilities for innovation and success.

In the following chapters, we will explore how you can choose the right no-code platform, design your app, monetize it, and successfully market it to your target audience. Let's get started!

Chapter 1: Understanding No-Code App Development

What is No-Code Development?

No-code development is a method of creating software applications without writing any code. It allows users to build apps using visual development tools, drag-and-drop elements, and pre-built functionalities. Instead of manually coding every aspect of an application, no-code platforms provide a simplified interface that abstracts the complexity of traditional programming, making app development accessible to non-technical users.

No-code platforms leverage pre-configured logic, integrations, and automation, allowing users to focus on their app's functionality rather than technical challenges. This democratization of software development has enabled entrepreneurs, small businesses, and enterprises to build and deploy applications quickly and cost-effectively.

How No-Code Differs from Traditional Coding

Traditional coding requires knowledge of programming languages such as Python, JavaScript, Swift, or Java. Developers write custom code to define an application's logic, user interface, and data management. This approach offers unlimited flexibility but also requires considerable time, skill, and resources.

No-code development, on the other hand, simplifies the process by providing:

- **Drag-and-Drop Interfaces** – Users can build app components visually rather than coding them from scratch.

- **Pre-Built Templates** – Many no-code platforms offer customizable templates to speed up development.
- **Automated Workflows** – Built-in logic and automation eliminate the need for writing backend code.
- **API Integrations** – Seamless connectivity with third-party services without manual coding.

While traditional coding offers greater control and customization, no-code platforms are ideal for those looking to quickly prototype, launch, or automate business processes without hiring a development team.

Best Use Cases for No-Code Apps

No-code platforms are best suited for applications that require rapid development and deployment without complex, custom functionality. Common use cases include:

1. **Business Process Automation** – Streamlining workflows for HR, finance, or customer support teams.
2. **Marketplace Apps** – Creating platforms that connect buyers and sellers.
3. **E-Commerce Stores** – Setting up online stores with product listings, payment gateways, and order management.
4. **Customer Relationship Management (CRM)** – Managing leads, sales pipelines, and customer interactions.
5. **Membership & Community Apps** – Building platforms for user engagement, such as forums or social networks.
6. **Educational Apps** – Delivering online courses, quizzes, and learning resources.
7. **Event Management Apps** – Organizing and coordinating events, ticketing, and attendee engagement.

By leveraging no-code platforms, businesses and individuals can quickly build functional applications tailored to their needs, reducing development costs and time-to-market.

In the next chapter, we will explore how to choose the right no-code platform based on your app idea and business goals.

Chapter 2: Choosing the Right No-Code Platform

Choosing the right no-code platform is crucial for transforming your app idea into a functional, user-friendly product. This chapter provides a comparison of top no-code app builders—Adalo, Bubble, Glide, Thunkable, and Softr—outlines key factors to consider when selecting a platform and discusses the differences between free and paid plans.

Comparison of Top No-Code App Builders

1. Adalo

Adalo enables users to create mobile and web applications with a focus on design flexibility. It offers a drag-and-drop interface, allowing for extensive customization. Users can publish apps directly to the Apple App Store and Google Play Store. Adalo's pricing starts at $45 per month.

adalo.com

2. Bubble

Bubble is known for its robust capabilities in building complex web applications. It provides a visual programming interface with a wide range of functionalities and integrations. Bubble offers extensive design freedom, making it suitable for highly customized applications. Pricing begins at $32 per month.

adalo.com

3. Glide

Glide transforms Google Sheets into mobile and web applications. It offers a streamlined design approach, which may limit full UI customization but ensures ease of use. Glide is ideal for simple applications and prototypes.

softr.io

4. Thunkable

Thunkable specializes in building native mobile apps for both iOS and Android platforms. It features a unique block-based system for app logic creation and a drag-and-drop interface for design. Pricing starts at $15 per month, but lower-tier plans may have limitations, such as a cap on monthly downloads and storage space.

adalo.com

5. Softr

Softr allows users to build web applications using Airtable as a database. It offers pre-built templates and components, making it accessible for users without design experience. Softr is suitable for creating membership sites, directories, and internal tools.

softr.io

Factors to Consider When Choosing a Platform

When selecting a no-code platform, consider the following factors:

1. **Project Requirements:** Determine the complexity of your app. For simple apps, platforms like Glide may suffice; for more complex functionalities, Bubble or Adalo might be more appropriate.
2. **Design Flexibility:** Assess the level of customization you need. Bubble offers extensive design freedom, while Glide provides a more streamlined approach.

3. **Platform Compatibility:** Ensure the platform supports your target devices. Thunkable is ideal for native mobile apps, whereas Softr focuses on web applications.
4. **Budget Constraints:** Consider the cost of the platform's plans and what features are included at each pricing tier.
5. **Scalability:** Evaluate whether the platform can handle your app's growth in terms of users and features.
6. **Integration Capabilities:** Check if the platform supports integration with other tools and services you plan to use.
7. **Learning Curve:** Some platforms may require more time to learn than others. Choose one that aligns with your technical comfort level.
8. **Community and Support:** A strong user community and support resources can be invaluable for troubleshooting and learning.

Free vs. Paid Plans

Most no-code platforms offer both free and paid plans, each with its own set of features and limitations.

Free Plans:

- Advantages:
  - Allow users to explore the platform and build prototypes without financial commitment.
  - Useful for learning and testing purposes.
- Limitations:
  - May include watermarks or branding on your app.
  - Limited features, storage, and user capacity.
  - Restrictions on publishing to app stores or using custom domains.

Paid Plans:

- Advantages:

- Access to advanced features and integrations.
  - Ability to publish apps without platform branding.
  - Increased storage, user capacity, and scalability options.
  - Priority support and access to premium resources.
- Considerations:
  - Costs vary between platforms; assess whether the features offered align with your project's needs and budget.

In summary, carefully evaluate your app's requirements, your technical skills, and your budget when choosing a no-code platform. Selecting the right platform will set the foundation for your app's success.

Note: Pricing and features are subject to change. Always refer to the official websites of the platforms for the most current information.

Chapter 3: Planning Your App Idea

Developing a successful app begins with a well-thought-out idea and meticulous planning. This chapter guides you through generating a profitable app concept, validating its market potential, and designing a foundational wireframe and user flow.

How to Come Up with a Profitable App Idea

1. **Identify Problems in Specific Industries:** Engage deeply with an industry that interests you. By understanding its nuances and challenges, you can pinpoint problems that lack efficient solutions. This immersion can reveal opportunities for innovative apps that address unmet needs.

   reddit.com

2. **Analyze Market Trends:** Stay informed about emerging technologies and consumer behaviors. For instance, the increasing adoption of AI in various sectors presents opportunities for apps that enhance efficiency and user experience.

   ft.com

3. **Explore Niche Markets:** Consider developing apps tailored to specific communities or needs. For example, creating a social networking app for single parents can foster connections and provide support, catering to a distinct user base.

   intelegain.com

4. **Enhance Existing Solutions:** Examine current apps and identify their shortcomings. Developing a more user-friendly or feature-rich version can attract users seeking better alternatives.

5. **Leverage Emerging Technologies:** Incorporate advancements like AI to create innovative applications. For example, AI-driven tools can assist in various tasks, such as drafting responses in customer service, thereby improving efficiency.

   ft.com

Validating Your Idea

Before investing time and resources into development, ensure there's a demand for your app:

1. **Market Research:**
   - Competitor Analysis: Identify existing apps similar to your concept. Analyze their features, user reviews, and market positioning to find gaps your app can fill.
   - Target Audience Identification: Define who your potential users are. Understanding their demographics and pain points helps tailor your app to their needs.
2. **Surveys and Interviews:**
   - Gather Feedback: Engage with your target audience through surveys or interviews to assess interest in your app idea. This direct feedback can validate your concept and provide insights for refinement. uptech.team
3. **Minimum Viable Product (MVP):**
   - Develop a Prototype: Create a simplified version of your app focusing on core functionalities. This allows you to test the concept with minimal investment.
   - Iterate Based on Feedback: Use user responses to refine and improve your app before full-scale development.

Creating a Wireframe and Basic User Flow

Visualizing your app's structure is a crucial step in the development process:

1. **Wireframing:**
   - Sketch the Layout: Draft basic screens to represent the app's interface. This helps in organizing content and functionalities logically.

- Focus on User Experience (UX): Ensure the design is intuitive, allowing users to navigate the app effortlessly.

2. **User Flow Diagram:**
   - Map User Journeys: Illustrate the steps a user takes to accomplish tasks within the app. This ensures that processes are streamlined and user-friendly.
   - Identify Potential Obstacles: Anticipate areas where users might face difficulties and adjust the design accordingly.

Utilizing tools like Adobe XD or Figma can aid in creating detailed wireframes and user flows, providing a clear blueprint for development.

By thoughtfully generating, validating, and planning your app idea, you lay a solid foundation for a product that resonates with users and stands out in the market.

Chapter 4: Building Your App Step-by-Step

Embarking on the journey of app development without traditional coding is both empowering and accessible, thanks to no-code platforms. This chapter provides a structured approach to building your app, covering platform setup, design principles, feature integration, and pre-launch testing.

Setting Up Your No-Code Platform

1. **Select the Appropriate Platform:**
   - Assess Your Needs: Determine the specific requirements of your app, such as the type of application (web or mobile), desired features, and scalability.
   - Platform Evaluation: Research and compare no-code platforms like Adalo, Bubble, Glide, Thunkable, and Softr to identify which aligns best with your project goals.
2. **Account Creation and Familiarization:**
   - Sign Up: Create an account on your chosen platform.
   - Explore Tutorials: Utilize available tutorials and documentation to familiarize yourself with the platform's interface and capabilities.
3. **Project Initialization:**
   - Start a New Project: Initiate a new project within the platform, selecting templates if available to expedite the development process.
   - Configure Settings: Set up essential configurations, including project name, supported devices, and any necessary integrations.

Designing Your App: UI/UX Basics

1. **User Interface (UI) Design:**

- Consistency: Maintain a uniform design language throughout the app to enhance user familiarity and comfort.
- Visual Hierarchy: Use size, color, and placement to prioritize information, guiding users' attention to key elements.
- Accessibility: Ensure that your design accommodates all users, including those with disabilities, by adhering to accessibility standards.

2. **User Experience (UX) Design:**
   - Intuitive Navigation: Design a straightforward and predictable navigation structure to facilitate easy movement within the app.
   - Feedback Mechanisms: Incorporate responses such as animations or messages to inform users about the outcomes of their actions.
   - Responsive Design: Optimize your app's performance and appearance across various devices and screen sizes.

3. **Prototyping Tools:**
   - Figma: A collaborative design tool that allows for real-time feedback and iteration.
   - Adobe XD: Offers a range of features for designing and prototyping user experiences.

Adding Essential Features

1. **Forms:**
   - Data Collection: Implement forms to gather user inputs, ensuring they are straightforward and user-friendly.
   - Validation: Incorporate real-time validation to assist users in providing correct information.

2. **Databases:**
   - Data Management: Set up databases to store and retrieve app data efficiently.
   - Integration: Ensure seamless connectivity between your app and the database for real-time data updates.

3. **Payment Systems:**

- Integration: Incorporate payment gateways like Stripe or PayPal to facilitate secure transactions.
- Security Compliance: Adhere to financial regulations and standards to protect user information.

4. **User Authentication:**
   - Access Control: Implement sign-up and login functionalities to manage user access and personalize experiences.
   - Security Measures: Utilize encryption and other security protocols to safeguard user data.

Evaluating Your App Before Launch

1. **Functional Testing:**
   - Feature Verification: Ensure all components of the app operate as intended.
   - User Scenarios: Test various user interactions to identify and rectify potential issues.

2. **Usability Testing:**
   - User Feedback: Conduct sessions with potential users to gather insights into the app's ease of use and overall experience.
   - Iterative Improvements: Refine the app based on feedback to enhance user satisfaction.

3. **Performance Testing:**
   - Load Handling: Assess the app's responsiveness under different conditions and user loads.
   - Optimization: Identify and address performance bottlenecks to ensure **smooth operation.**

4. **Cross-Platform Testing:**
   - Device Compatibility: Verify that the app functions correctly across various devices and operating systems.
   - Browser Compatibility: Ensure consistent performance on different web browsers, if applicable.

By meticulously following these steps, you can develop a robust, user-friendly app without the need for traditional coding skills. Leveraging no-code platforms democratizes app development, enabling innovative solutions to emerge from diverse creators.

Chapter 5: Monetizing Your App

Monetizing your app effectively is crucial to ensure its sustainability and profitability. This chapter explores various monetization strategies, guides you on pricing your app for success, and provides insights into setting up payment gateways like Stripe and PayPal.

Different Ways to Make Money from Your App

1. **In-App Advertising:**
   - Description: Displaying ads within your app.
   - Types of Ads:
     - Banner Ads: Static or dynamic ads displayed at the top or bottom of the screen.
     - Interstitial Ads: Full-screen ads that appear at natural transition points, such as between levels in a game.
     - Native Ads: Ads that match the look and feel of your app's content, providing a seamless user experience.
   - Considerations: Ensure ads are relevant and non-intrusive to maintain a positive user experience.
     admob.google.com
2. **In-App Purchases (IAPs):**
   - Description: Selling virtual goods or premium features within the app.
   - Types:
     - Consumable: Items that can be used once, such as virtual currency or extra lives.
     - Non-Consumable: Permanent features or content, like ad removal or additional levels.
   - Considerations: Clearly communicate the value of in-app purchases to users.
     adapty.io
3. **Subscriptions:**

- Description: Charging users a recurring fee to access content or features.
- Models:
  - Freemium: Offering basic features for free, with premium features available through subscription.
  - Premium: Providing all content exclusively to subscribers.
- Consideration: Offer valuable and regularly updated content to justify recurring payments.

4. **Paid App Downloads:**
   - Description: Charging users a one-time fee to download the app.
   - Considerations: This model works best if your app offers unique value not readily available in free apps.

5. **Sponsorships and Partnerships:**
   - Description: Collaborating with brands to offer sponsored content or features.
   - Considerations: Ensure that sponsored content aligns with your app's purpose and audience interests.

How to Price Your App for Success

1. **Research the Market:**
   - Competitor Analysis: Examine similar apps to understand their pricing models and user reception.
   - User Demographics: Assess your target audience's willingness to pay and their spending habits.

2. **Determine Your Value Proposition:**
   - Unique Features: Highlight what sets your app apart and price accordingly.
   - Cost-Benefit Analysis: Ensure the price reflects the value and benefits provided to the user.

3. **Choose a Pricing Strategy:**
   - Penetration Pricing: Starting with a lower price to attract users, then gradually increasing it.

- Premium Pricing: Setting a higher price to reflect exclusivity or superior quality.
- Psychological Pricing: Using pricing tactics like $0.99 instead of $1.00 to make the price seem lower.

4. **Test and Iterate:**
   - A/B Testing: Experiment with different price points to see which yields the best results.
   - Gather Feedback: Listen to user feedback regarding pricing and adjust as necessary.

Setting Up Payment Gateways

1. **Choose a Payment Gateway:**
   - Popular Options: Stripe and PayPal are widely used due to their robust features and ease of integration.
   - Considerations:
     - Transaction Fees: Understand the cost per transaction and any additional fees.
     - Supported Countries and Currencies: Ensure the gateway supports transactions in your target regions.
     - Security Features: Look for gateways that offer strong fraud protection and compliance with standards like PCI DSS.

2. **Integrate the Payment Gateway into Your App:**
   - Utilize SDKs: Many payment gateways offer Software Development Kits (SDKs) that simplify the integration process.
   - Follow Documentation: Adhere to the gateway integration guides to ensure proper setup.
   - Testing: Before going live, test the payment process in a sandbox environment to identify and fix any issues.

     weareplanet.com

3. **Ensure Compliance and Security:**

- Data Encryption: Implement SSL certificates to protect user data during transactions.
- Regular Audits: Conduct security audits to identify and address vulnerabilities.
- Compliance: Stay updated with financial regulations and ensure your app adheres to necessary compliance standards.

By thoughtfully selecting monetization strategies, pricing your app appropriately, and integrating secure payment gateways, you can create a sustainable revenue stream while providing value to your users.

Chapter 6: Publishing Your App

Publishing your app is a pivotal step in bringing your creation to users worldwide. This chapter provides a comprehensive guide on submitting your app to the Apple App Store and Google Play Store, highlights common reasons for rejection and how to avoid them, and explores alternative distribution methods.

How to Submit Your App to the Apple App Store

1. **Enroll in the Apple Developer Program:**
   - Requirement: A paid Apple Developer account is necessary to distribute apps on the App Store.
   - Process: Visit the Apple Developer Program enrollment page and follow the instructions to enroll.

2. **Prepare Your App for Submission:**
   - Testing: Ensure your app is free of bugs and performs optimally across all supported devices.
   - App Information: Gather essential details such as app name, icon, description, screenshots, and a privacy policy URL.

3. **Create an App Store Connect Record:**
   - Access: Log in to App Store Connect.
   - Add New App: Navigate to "My Apps," click the "+" sign, and select "New App." Provide the required information, including platform, app name, primary language, bundle ID, and SKU.

4. **Upload Your App Using Xcode:**
   - Archive the App: In Xcode, select your project, choose "Generic iOS Device" as the deployment target, then select "Product" > "Archive."
   - Upload: Once the archive is created, click "Distribute App," select the App Store, and follow the prompts to upload your app.

5. **Submit for Review:**

- Complete App Information: In App Store Connect, enter all necessary information, including pricing and availability.
- Submit: After completing all fields and uploading the build, click "Submit for Review."

For detailed guidance, refer to Apple's official documentation on submitting iOS apps.

How to Submit Your App to the Google Play Store

1. **Enrolling in the Google Play Developer Program:**
   - Requirement: A Google Play Developer account is required to distribute apps on the Play Store.
   - Process: Sign up at the Google Play Console and pay the one-time registration fee.
2. **Prepare Your App for Submission:**
   - Testing: Ensure your app is thoroughly tested and free of issues.
   - App Bundle/APK: Generate a signed app bundle or APK using Android Studio.
3. **Create a Google Play Console Entry:**
   - Access: Log in to the Google Play Console.
   - Add a New App: Click "Create App," and provide the necessary details, including app name, default language, and app or game designation.
4. **Prepare Store Listing:**
   - App Details: Enter information such as app description, screenshots, icons, and categorization.
5. **Upload Your App Bundle/APK:**
   - Release Management: Navigate to "Production" > "Create New Release," and upload your app bundle or APK.
6. **Set Up Content Rating, Pricing, and Distribution:**
   - Content Rating: Complete the content rating questionnaire.
   - Pricing: Specify whether your app is free or paid and select the countries where it will be available.
7. **Review and Publish:**

- o Review: Ensure all sections are complete and accurate.
- o Publish: Click "Publish" to submit your app for review.

For a step-by-step guide, consult Google Play Console Help.

Common Reasons for Rejection and How to Avoid Them

1. **Crashes and Bugs:**
   - o Issue: Apps that crash or contain significant bugs are often rejected.
   - o Solution: Conduct extensive testing on multiple devices and OS versions to ensure stability.
2. **Poor Performance:**
   - o Issue: Slow load times or unresponsive interfaces can lead to rejection.
   - o Solution: Optimize your app's performance and ensure a smooth user experience.
3. **Privacy Concerns:**
   - o Issue: Non-compliance with privacy policies, such as unauthorized data collection, can result in rejection.
   - o Solution: Clearly disclose data usage practices and obtain necessary user permissions.
4. **Copycat Designs:**
   - o Issue: Apps that closely mimic existing ones may be rejected for lack of originality.
   - o Solution: Ensure your app offers unique features or content that differentiates it from others.
5. **Broken Links:**
   - o Issue: In-app links that lead to non-existent pages or errors can cause rejection.
   - o Solution: Regularly assess all links within your app to ensure they function correctly.
6. **Incomplete Information:**

- ○ Issue: Missing or inaccurate app information can delay approval.
- ○ Solution: Provide comprehensive and accurate details in your app's metadata and store listing.

For more insights, refer to <u>Adapty's guide on App Store rejections</u> and <u>MobiLoud's article on common rejection reasons</u>.

Chapter 7: Marketing & Selling Your App

Marketing and selling your app effectively are crucial to its success in a competitive marketplace. This chapter outlines strategies to create a robust launch plan, optimize your app's presence in stores, and leverage various marketing channels to maximize reach and revenue.

Creating a Launch Strategy

1. Pre-Launch Preparation:
   - Market Research: Identify your target audience and analyze competitors to understand market needs and positioning.
   - Online Presence: Establish a dedicated website and social media profiles to build awareness and engage potential users.
2. Soft Launch:
   - Beta Testing: Release a beta version to a limited audience to gather feedback and identify issues before the official launch.
3. Official Launch:
   - Press Releases: Distribute press releases to relevant media outlets to announce your app's availability.
   - Launch Events: Host virtual or physical events to generate buzz and attract users.

App Store Optimization (ASO) to Boost Downloads

1. Keyword Optimization:
   - Research: Identify relevant keywords that potential users are likely to search for.

- Implementation: Incorporate these keywords into your app's title, description, and metadata to improve visibility.
2. **Visual Assets:**
    - App Icon: Design a distinctive and appealing icon that captures the essence of your app.
    - Screenshots and Videos: Use high-quality images and videos to display your app's features and benefits.
3. **User Reviews and Ratings:**
    - Encourage Feedback: Prompt satisfied users to leave positive reviews.
    - Respond to Reviews: Engage with users by addressing their feedback, demonstrating commitment to improvement.

For a comprehensive guide on ASO strategies, refer to the Business of Apps article.

Paid vs. Organic Marketing Strategies

1. **Organic Strategies:**
    - Content Marketing: Create valuable content related to your app's niche to attract and engage users.
    - Social Media Engagement: Utilize platforms like Instagram, Twitter, and TikTok to build a community and promote your app.
    - Search Engine Optimization (SEO): Optimize your website and content to rank higher in search engine results, increasing organic traffic.
2. **Paid Strategies:**
    - Social Media Advertising: Run targeted ads on platforms where your potential users are most active.
    - Influencer Partnerships: Collaborate with influencers to reach a broader audience and build credibility.
    - Paid Search Ads: Utilize services like Google Ads to appear in search results for relevant keywords.

Balancing both paid and organic strategies can enhance visibility and user acquisition.

Using Affiliate Marketing and Partnerships

1. **Affiliate Marketing:**
   - Program Development: Create an affiliate program where partners earn a commission for referring inexperienced users.
   - Partner Selection: Choose affiliates whose audience aligns with your target market to ensure quality leads.
2. **Strategic Partnerships:**
   - Co-Branding: Collaborate with complementary apps or services to offer bundled promotions.
   - Exclusive Launch Partners: Partner with established brands to leverage their audience during your app's launch.

For example, Tesco Finest partnered with The Guardian's Feast app to enhance brand visibility and user engagement. theguardian.com

Implementing these strategies thoughtfully can significantly impact your app's success in the market. Continuous analysis and adaptation of your marketing efforts will help maintain growth and user retention.

Chapter 8: Scaling and Growing Your App Business

Scaling and growing your app business involves strategic planning, effective user acquisition, operational efficiency, and knowing when to seek additional expertise or consider an escape plan. This chapter provides insights into acquiring your first 1,000 users, scaling through automation and integrations, hiring developers when necessary, and options for selling your app.

Acquiring Your First 1,000 Users

1. **Leverage Personal Networks:**
   - Outreach: Share your app within your personal and professional circles through social media, email, and direct communication. Personal endorsements can lead to initial user adoption.
2. **Engage in Community Building:**
   - Online Forums and Groups: Participate in communities related to your app's niche. Offer value through insights and subtly introduce your app as a solution to common problems.
   - Feedback Solicitation: Encourage early adopters to provide feedback, fostering a sense of involvement and loyalty.
3. **Implement Referral Programs:**
   - Incentivize Sharing: Offer rewards or premium features to users who refer others, creating a viral loop that encourages organic growth.
4. **Utilize Content Marketing:**
   - Educational Content: Create blogs, videos, or podcasts that address topics relevant to your target audience, positioning your app as a valuable resource.
5. **Collaborate with Influencers:**

- Partnerships: Work with influencers whose followers align with your target market to gain credibility and expand reach.

For additional strategies, consider insights from Draftbit and Appfigures.

Scaling with Automation and Integrations

1. **Automate Repetitive Tasks:**
   - Marketing Automation: Use tools to schedule social media posts, manage email campaigns, and track user engagement, freeing up time for strategic activities.
   - Customer Support: Implement chatbots and automated response systems to manage common inquiries efficiently.
2. **Integrate Third-Party Services:**
   - Analytics Platforms: Incorporate services like Google Analytics or Mixpanel to monitor user behavior and app performance.
   - Payment Gateways: Use trusted payment processors such as Stripe or PayPal to manage transactions securely and efficiently.
3. **Enhance User Experience:**
   - Personalization: Utilize data to tailor content and recommendations to individual users, increasing engagement and retention.

Hiring Developers: When and How

1. **Identifying the Need:**
   - Technical Limitations: If your app requires complex features beyond your expertise or existing platform capabilities, it may be time to hire a developer.
   - Scalability Challenges: As your user base grows, ensuring the app can manage increased traffic and data may necessitate professional development skills.

2. **Hiring Options:**
   - Freelance Developers: Ideal for short-term projects or specific tasks. Platforms like Upwork or Freelancer can connect you with qualified professionals.
   - Development Agencies: Offer a team of experts for comprehensive app development needs, suitable for larger projects.
   - In-House Developers: Hiring full-time developers provides dedicated resources beneficial for ongoing development and maintenance.
3. **Selection Criteria:**
   - Experience and Portfolio: Review past projects to assess their capability in handling similar tasks.
   - Technical Proficiency: Ensure they are skilled in the necessary programming languages and tools relevant to your app.
   - Cultural Fit: Aligning with your company's values and work style can lead to more cohesive collaboration.

Selling Your App: Platforms and Considerations

1. **Flippa:**
   - Overview: A marketplace for buying and selling online businesses, including apps.
   - Process: List your app, provide detailed information, and engage with potential buyers through the platform.
   - Considerations: Flippa caters for a wide range of businesses, which can lead to varied buyer interest.
2. **Acquire.com (formerly MicroAcquire):**
   - Overview: Specializes in startup acquisitions, focusing on SaaS businesses, e-commerce, and mobile apps.
   - Process: Create a profile for your app, highlight key metrics, and connect with vetted buyers.
   - Considerations: Acquire.com offers a more curated marketplace, potentially leading to higher-quality engagements.

3. **Private Buyers:**
    - Direct Outreach: Network within industry circles or use professional platforms like LinkedIn to find interested parties.
    - Brokers: Engage intermediaries who can connect you with potential buyers and assist in negotiations.

Key Considerations Before Selling:

- **Valuation:** Assess your app's worth based on revenue, user base, growth potential, and market trends.
- **Due Diligence:** Prepare comprehensive documentation, including financial records, user metrics, and intellectual property rights.
- **Post-Sale Obligations:** Understand any commitments required after the sale, such as transition support or non-compete clauses.

For more insights on selling your app, refer to Flippa's guide and comparisons between Flippa and Acquire.

By focusing on strategic user acquisition, leveraging automation, knowing when to expand your team, and understanding the avenues for selling your app, you can effectively scale and grow your app business.

Conclusion

Embarking on the journey of building and scaling a no-code app is both exciting and challenging. This guide has equipped you with the foundational knowledge to transform your app idea into a reality without traditional coding. Let us recap the key takeaways and explore strategies for continuous improvement and further learning.

Key Takeaways

1. **Embrace No-Code Platforms:** Leverage tools like Adalo, Bubble, Glide, Thunkable, and Softr to design and develop apps efficiently without coding expertise.
2. **Strategic Planning:** Invest time in market research, idea validation, and wireframing to ensure your app addresses real user needs and stands out in the market.
3. **User-Centric Design:** Focus on intuitive UI/UX design to enhance user engagement and satisfaction.
4. **Monetization Strategies:** Explore various revenue models such as subscriptions, in-app purchases, and ads to generate income from your app.
5. **Effective Marketing:** Utilize both organic and paid marketing strategies, including social media engagement, influencer partnerships, and App Store Optimization (ASO), to reach and grow your user base.
6. **Continuous Improvement:** Regularly update your app based on user feedback and analytics to maintain relevance and competitiveness.

Post-Launch Improvement Strategies

1. Analyze User Behavior:

- Data-Driven Decisions: Utilize analytics tools to monitor how users interact with your app, identifying popular features and areas needing enhancement.
- Feedback Loops: Encourage users to provide feedback through in-app surveys or reviews, fostering a community invested in your app's evolution.

2. **Regular Updates and Enhancements:**
   - Feature Expansion: Introduce new functionalities that align with user needs and market trends to keep the app engaging.
   - Performance Optimization: Continuously improve app speed, fix bugs, and ensure compatibility with the latest devices and operating systems.

3. **Community Engagement:**
   - Build a User Community: Create forums or social media groups where users can share experiences, suggest features, and assist each other.
   - Transparent Communication: Keep users informed about upcoming updates, maintenance schedules, and new features to build trust and loyalty.

4. **Leverage Automation and Integrations:**
   - Automate Marketing Efforts: Use tools to schedule social media posts, manage email campaigns, and track user engagement efficiently.
   - Integrate Third-Party Services: Enhance functionality by incorporating services like payment gateways, analytics platforms, and customer support systems.

Additional Resources for Further Learning

1. **No-Code Learning Platforms:**
   - Noloco's Beginner's Guide: Offers comprehensive tutorials and insights into no-code app development.
     noloco.io
   - Devlin Peck's No-Code Tools for eLearning: Explores various no-code tools suitable for creating educational applications.
     devlinpeck.com

2. **Community Forums and Groups:**
   - Reddit's r/nocode: A community where no-code enthusiasts share experiences, resources, and support.

     reddit.com
   - No Code Founders: A platform connecting no-code entrepreneurs, offering resources and networking opportunities.
3. **Educational Content:**
   - Medium Articles: In-depth articles covering various aspects of no-code development and app marketing strategies.

     medium.com
   - Adalo Blog: Features tutorials, case studies, and tips for building apps using Adalo and other no-code platforms.

     adalo.com

Remember, the success of your app hinges on continuous learning, adaptation, and a deep understanding of your users' evolving needs. Stay curious, engage with the no-code community, and keep refining your skills to navigate the dynamic landscape of app development successfully.

Reference

1. No-Code Development Platforms:

- Bubble.io: A comprehensive platform enabling users to build full-stack web applications through visual programming.
- Thunkable: Specializes in mobile app development, offering a drag-and-drop interface to create native apps for iOS and Android.
  thunkable.com
- AppSheet by Google Cloud: Empowers users to build powerful applications directly from data sources like Google Sheets and Excel without coding.
  cloud.google.com
- Adalo: Enables the creation of interactive and database-driven applications with ease.
  adalo.com

2. Educational Resources and Communities:

- NoCode.Tech: A leading educational platform offering tutorials, templates, and a community forum to assist no-code developers.
  nocode.tech
- Reddit's r/Entrepreneur: A community where entrepreneurs share insights, including guides on building apps without code.
  reddit.com

3. Success Stories and Case Studies:

- AirDev's No-Code App Examples: Showcases a variety of applications built by startups and businesses using no-code tools, providing inspiration and practical insights.
  airdev.co
- NoCodeExits: Features over 50 success stories of entrepreneurs who have built and scaled applications without traditional coding.
  nocodeexits.com

- Nomtek's No-Code Startups: Highlights successful companies that have leveraged no-code platforms to launch and grow their businesses.
  nomtek.com

4. Comprehensive Guides and Articles:

- Zapier's Best No-Code App Builders in 2025: Provides an in-depth analysis of top no-code platforms, helping you choose the right tool for your project.
  zapier.com
- Medium's No-Code Startups Making Over $1M in Revenue: Explores how entrepreneurs have successfully built profitable startups using no-code solutions.
  medium.com